Striving and Thriving

Meeting the Challenges of Change

Striving and Thriving

Meeting the Challenges of Change

Daniel H. Johnston, Ph.D.

A Lessons for Living Book

Dagali Press
5663 Taylor Terrace
Macon, Georgia 31210

Dagali Press, 5663 Taylor Terrace, Macon, Georgia 31210
Phone: (478) 471-1008
E-mail: dagalipress@lessonsforliving.com

FIRST EDITION
First Printing, 2004

Library of Congress Control Number: 2003096583
ISBN: 0-9712165-1-7

Cover photo by Dan Johnston

Disclaimer

The purpose of this book is to educate and entertain. The author
will have no liability or responsibility to any person(s) or entity
with respect to any alleged loss or damage caused either direct-
ly or indirectly by information contained in the book. Readers
should consult a health care professional if they have questions
regarding the information included in this book especially as it
relates to individual concerns regarding mental, emotional, and
physical health.

Life belongs to the living, and he who lives must be prepared for change.

~ Johann von Goethe

Table of Contents

We change, whether we like it or not.
~ Ralph Waldo Emerson

Introduction

In 1994, when asked by the administrator of the information services department of the hospital where I worked to design a workshop on change management to help prepare her staff for some coming organizational changes, I declined the request. At the time, I thought that I did not know enough about how change worked.

A few days later, however, I was struck by the obvious facts that as a psychologist I helped people to change all the time, and that individual change might not be that different from organizational change. I agreed to develop a short seminar on adapting to change.

As a result of this initial effort, I was later appointed to lead a change management team with the mission of developing an educational program on understanding change that could be offered to all employees. The goal was to facilitate the acceptance of a redesigned service delivery system by teaching fundamental coping skills in the context of a general model of how change worked in daily life.

Since my involvement in the early days of this project, I have continued to refine a basic change management model that explains the six fundamental steps of change, as well as the typical emotions of the change process. Also incorporated into this model are the two central features of resistance and resiliency.

While resistance to change always occurs, it can be helpful when properly understood as offering useful information rather than just viewed as a devious attempt to undercut the process.

Resiliency is a valuable set of skills that helps people to not only bounce back from the ups and downs of change but to move forward with change in a positive direction. It is resiliency that enables people to do more than just survive the process. Resiliency makes striving and thriving possible in the face of change.

Striving refers to making an intentional, goal directed effort at confronting and overcoming the challenges faced. It requires the ability to develop and maintain a realistically positive attitude while managing the ongoing stress of living with change. It is an individual choice that can be aided by education and training.

Thriving is the ability to sustain progress toward a goal despite circumstances faced. People who thrive on change are able to find enjoyment in the process by focusing on a sense of accomplishment while maintaining an appropriate balance of meaning and purpose in their lives.

This book presents a model of the change process that teaches people how to go from just trying to survive change to being able to strive and thrive through it. The goal is to help develop change-ability: The ability to design, implement, and follow through with effective strategies of change management.

The Changing Nature of Change

◆ Do you encounter more change than in the past?
◆ Does change seem never ending?
◆ Would you like to manage change better?
◆ Do you need to help others cope with change?
◆ Would you like to build a resilient work force?

If any of these questions catch your attention, you must be confronting the challenges of change. It is vitally important to understand that change is nothing more than the natural order of things. It is a normal process that will always be with us. Without change, life would be boring. Change in itself is not the problem.

The early Greek philosophers were interested in change. One of them, Heraclitus, claimed, "You cannot step into the same river twice." When you think about it, the truth of this statement is obvious. In the time it takes to put one foot and then the other into the river, the water has been flowing and changing. In a similar manner, everything around us is always moving, flowing, and changing.

Heraclitus also declared, "Change alone is unchanging." He was both right and wrong.

Change is unchanging in that it is constant and always present. The nature of change, however, has changed. The frequency and variety of changing events has become faster than ever before in history. Furthermore, each day the rate of change continues to accelerate, and it will not slow down again.

The somewhat shocking truth is that we are currently living in what we will soon come to call "The Good Old Days." In a few years we will look back on today as the time when there was stability, predictability, and things stayed the same for a reasonable length of time. We will come to experience a nostalgic longing for a return to this time when change was slow.

If it seems to you that the challenge of change has itself become more challenging, you are right!

The Speed of Change

Let us examine what has happened to the speed of change by reviewing two examples: (1) the speed of transportation and (2) the acceleration of knowledge.

Around 6000 B.C., the camel caravan was the fastest form of transportation with an average rate of about eight miles per hour. In the late 18th century (around 1785 A.D.) the stagecoach, with newly improved wheels, was able to cover about 10 miles per hour. It had taken mankind about 8,000 years to raise the average speed of travel by two miles per hour. Forty years later in 1825, the steam engine was invented and within a decade locomotives could carry people at a speed of 13 miles per hour. In the short span of five decades the average rate of speed had increased more than in the previous 8,000 years. Within the next one hundred years airplanes were going 100 miles per hour and by the year 1960 missiles were traveling at over 1,800 miles per hour. Today the space shuttle car-ries its passengers around the world at speeds of five miles per second or 17,500 miles per hour. The rapid acceleration in the speed of transportation has transformed our planet bringing tremendous change in its wake.

The "change" of the rate of change is also evident when we ask, "How quickly does what we know increase?" French sociologist Georges Anderlas studied this question in the early 1970s. He made the fundamental assumption that all of the philosophical and scientific knowledge which mankind had accumulated by the year 1 A.D. equaled what he labeled as a "Unit of Information." Anderlas wondered how long it took that one "Unit" to double. He determined the answer to be 1,500 years or until the 16th century.

The next doubling of information, from two to four Units, took only 250 years or up until 1750. By 1900, only 150 years later, information had doubled again up to eight Units. The speed of doubling was getting faster and faster.

Sixteen Units of Information were reached in 1950 with the passage of only 50 years, and this doubled again in just 10 years to a total of 32 Units. Another seven years and it was at 64 Units, and then in just six years, the total had reached 128 Units of Information. This was in 1973, the year Anderlas' study ended. The doubling speed of information has continued to accelerate and is now estimated to occur about every 18 months. With the coming of the Internet, information in certain specialized areas may double every year.

Living in such an explosion of knowledge, it is no wonder you have a hard time keeping up. Often, trying to stay abreast with the knowledge base of just a limited area of interest is nearly impossible. When you move out of this familiar area, sorting through the ever-widening maze of information is mind-boggling. As people struggle with an increasing avalanche of data, they try to control and limit the size of the information pool with which they must be familiar, and as a result more and more specialization of interests is seen.

Change and the Information Age

To assist in managing all of this information, we have computers; the same computers that helped to create the huge mass of knowledge. Not surprisingly, computer technology demonstrates its own rapid acceleration of change as is most evident in what is known as Moore's Law.

In 1966, Gordon Moore, the founder of the computer chip maker Intel, declared that the power and complexity of the silicon chip would double every 12-18 months. This 18-month prediction has proven true, and today's computer chip is millions of times as powerful as its predecessor of the 1960s. These robust processors have ushered us into the Information Age as they manipulate, sort, and collate ever-increasing amounts of data. As a consequence, new products, inventions, procedures, and policies (all based on rapidly available information) are announced every day, while change continues speeding ahead.

Having moved out of the Industrial Age into the Information Age, we are confronting continual adjustments to new and different situations. Hundreds of channels on satellite and cable TV bombard us with sensory and information overload, and 24 hour news stations update us every 30 minutes. With the simple act of listening to the evening news, we learn all of the major events of the day from around the world.

As a member of the Global Village, you learn almost instantaneously what in the past would have taken months or years to learn. The result is that you are immediately impacted by a wide variety of world events, most of which seem to be "bad" news of crime, violence, and political conflict. Economic problems, downsizing, restructuring, and re-engineering threaten formerly secure jobs as family life is thrown into turmoil.

Safe havens from change are only temporarily found, perhaps while on a vacation or in a quiet stolen moment as you admire the beauty of a flower garden from your office window. Such moments of peace and serenity are often missing from modern life because the rules are always changing, and it is becoming harder and harder to predict what will happen next.

Recent psychological studies have suggested the need for a new diagnostic category of "information fatigue syndrome" to describe what occurs when you encounter more information than you can handle. In modern society, we are receiving information at 400 times the rate of the "Renaissance Man." One issue of the *New York Times* (or any Sunday edition of a large metropolitan newspaper) contains all the information that a 17th century-person would assimilate in a lifetime. Upper level managers in Fortune 500 companies must read about one million words a week to keep up. They receive an average of 180 voice, fax, e-mail, and pager messages per day. At one-minute per message, it takes about three hours of the day just to stay in touch.

Computer technology, the information highway, and the Internet are creating something new: techno-stress. Techo-stress is the stress of continually adjusting to novel technologies.

There is also the recent concept of "time sickness," which comes from trying to juggle too many options with too little time. We are experiencing events happening faster and faster, and it is difficult for us to slow down. We actually become impatient with the "slower computers" (which are in fact amazingly fast) when we have to wait that extra few seconds for something to happen. Frustration and stress arrive as we wait for the monitor screen to change. Alvin Toffler's long predicted "Future Shock" (too much change in too short of a time) has arrived.

Too Slow, Too Fast, Just Right

When confronting change there are three possibilities. The rate of change may be too slow, too fast, or just right. If change is too slow, you may find yourself bored with a lack of motivation and drive. When change is too fast, you are at risk for Future Shock or burnout. If, however, you can find and manage the "just-right," optimal level of change, it places you at the cutting edge of motivation, creativity, and choice.

In the current whirlwind of change, finding that cutting edge of creativity can be difficult because when a new change enters your life, it may first appear as a crisis. At these times, it is vital to know that a crisis can represent much more than just danger.

The Dangerous Opportunity

The Chinese ideogram for the English word crisis is composed of two separate characters: one means danger and the other means opportunity. The proper translation is that a crisis is a dangerous opportunity. This is always true; and when confronting any crisis situation, it is best to recognize both aspects. Unfortunately, we are hindered in doing so because human nature requires us to be "danger people."

Evolutionary history has dictated that when something new enters the environment, we must quickly scan it for threat. Survival of the species relies upon recognizing and avoiding danger. The result is that with the appearance of change, danger is readily seen and any opportunity can be well hidden. To effectively engage change, we must learn to search out the opportunity as well as respond to the danger.

If you examine your reactions to change, you will probably find a typical response pattern of being either a danger person or an opportunity person.

Knowing your pattern is helpful and can sensitize you to exercising caution, so you can control your response to change rather than be controlled by it.

You may find different reactions in different settings. At work you might always see danger, while at home change usually signals opportunity. Knowing your typical style is useful information because once you know your style, you can open yourself to the opposite tendency and ensure the consideration of both dangers and opportunities.

Through the process of intentionally challenging yourself to look for the positive in a crisis, it is possible to become an "opportunity person." Being an opportunity person is a choice, and it is one that enhances your ability to successfully handle change.

How well you live with change can also be made even less of a crisis if you understand the cycle of change and how it works.

The Six-Step Cycle of Change

The Six-Step Cycle of Change

Change can be conceptualized as a six-step, repeating process with two central features of resistance and resiliency. A working knowledge of the change cycle makes change easier to plan, lead, and follow.

The first step of the change process involves early recognition that change is coming. It is the phase when, with everything going well and feeling normal, you begin to get the eerie sensation that something is different. It can be hard to put your finger on and may be only a vague awareness, but you know that change is approaching. You sense: "Something's up."

It is as if you are standing on a beach feeling safe while being totally unaware that a tidal wave is rushing toward shore. There may be some warning signs that an astute observer could spot. Perhaps a weather pattern, cloud formation, or barometer reading would give a clue. A subtle pattern of seemingly random events exists, which if recognized would signal the approaching event. Someone recognizing the pattern could raise the alarm about what is coming and get a head start on preparation.

The importance of early recognition is illustrated in a child's riddle.

One day a large lake contains only a single, small lily pad. Each day the number of lily pads doubles, until on the 30th day the lake is full of lily pads. On which day was the lake half full?

The answer is on the 29th day.

Consider how the lake looked on the 29th day. Since it was only half full of lily pads, if you wanted to go swimming, you could. You could go boating if you so desired. There was still plenty of room. Fishing was also possible. The very next day, however, disaster had struck. The lake was choked with lily pads. No space for swimming or boating could be found, and the fish were dying.

Early recognition of the doubling pattern of the lilies could have enabled an appropriate intervention. Now, however, it was too late. Change had struck. The daily doubling of lily pads should have raised some concerns because a disaster was coming.

To better understand this process, let us review the six steps of change using examples from both personal life and a work setting.

As we do so, recall a recent change in your life (perhaps a move, job change, or a child leaving home) and see how it fits this model. Try to identify what you did at each step.

The Six-Step Cycle of Change

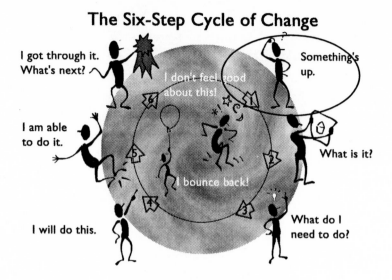

Step One: Something's up.

The first stage of change involves an intuitive recognition that change is coming.

Examples of Personal Change for Step One

Let's consider the commonly experienced personal change of pregnancy. How do you know if you or someone you care about is pregnant? Early signs might be:

- ◆ Nausea in the morning
- ◆ Weight gain
- ◆ Moodiness
- ◆ Food craving

Imagine that you are a woman waking up one morning feeling nauseated. Do you decide that you are pregnant? What if one day you are moody? Do you decide that you are pregnant? What if you notice weight gain? Do you decide now?

If each observation is isolated, the answer is "No." But, what if you notice all three events and several have happened more than once? Now you might begin to consider the possibility, "Something's up." You could be pregnant. With awareness of this possibility you move to step two of the change cycle and try to clearly define what is happening.

Examples of Work Related Change for Step One:

Change in the workplace also follows the six-step cycle.

Observations are made that signal coming change, and awareness develops that "Something's up."

Health care provides an example of this process. When managed health care was a phenomenon sweeping across the country, its arrival in a community wrought tremendous changes on the major service providers. Capitation and contracts pushed revenues down while a demand for quality service remained high. The result was that many hospitals across the country fell into financial hard times of downsizing. Some hospitals were forced to close.

Administrators noticing this trend in news reports from different areas of the nation could easily predict that managed care would eventually reach their location with the same effect. Sensing "Something's up" and seeking clarification, they advance to step two of the change cycle.

The Six-Step Cycle of Change

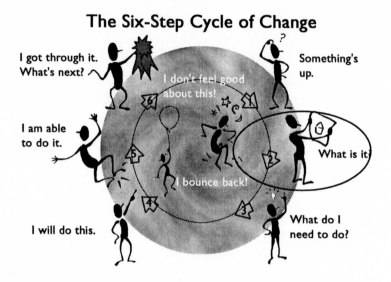

Step Two: What is it?

S tep two of the cycle of change is one of clarifying and clearly defining the situation. The goal is to identify and describe the issues confronting you so that they can be assessed for danger and opportunity. A clear understanding of the situation is needed in order to determine the best course of action.

Examples of Personal Change for Step Two

When pregnancy is suspected, a pregnancy test is needed, and the results will unambiguously indicate yes or no.

If the test is positive, you may now look back and think, "I should have known." With hindsight, the early warning signs are obvious.

When the answer is yes and the situation is clearly recognized, you face the task of deciding what to do next. You need a plan of action.

Examples of Work Related Change for Step Two

With enough information from early trend indicators, you are able to formulate a statement of the situation. For a hospital facing the impact of a competitive business environment, it might be:

"Service delivery must be streamlined so that it is more efficient and cost effective while, at the same time, maintaining the highest quality clinical service."

Such a clear statement of the problem forms the foundation for preparing for managed care's arrival in your community.

You must now plan what to do.

The Six-Step Cycle of Change

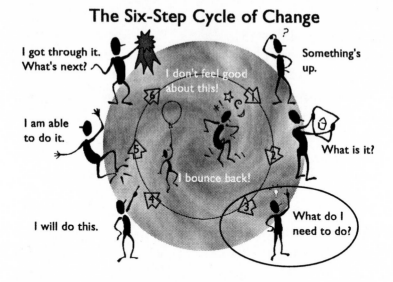

Step Three: What do I need to do?

Once the situation is clearly identified, a plan of action is required to identify what needs to be done and to determine who will do it. Technically speaking, this is an implementation plan, and while it may be formal or informal, it must be developed.

Examples of Personal Change for Step Three

If you are pregnant and looking ahead to the next nine months, what needs to be done? A number of questions arise:

- ◆ What doctor will you use?
- ◆ How will you afford the expense?
- ◆ What is your employer's family leave policy?
- ◆ Do you have enough room for a nursery?
- ◆ What furnishings do you need?
- ◆ Will you take childbirth classes?

Answering all of these questions and putting them in some sequence will create an action plan. With well-developed answers, you will know what to do. Next, you just do what you have planned.

Examples of Work Related Change for Step Three

With a clear statement of the opportunity, you must now create a plan of action. A system wide redesign of service delivery may be needed. Several planning teams consisting of a variety of workers are gathered together and told to design the ideal patient care system by developing specific, detailed implementation plans that answer these questions:

◆   What must be done?
◆   Who will do it?
◆   What job roles change?
◆   How much will it cost?
◆   Will quality of care improve?
◆   How long will it take?

With the formulation of a detailed implementation plan, you are ready to act.

The Six-Step Cycle of Change

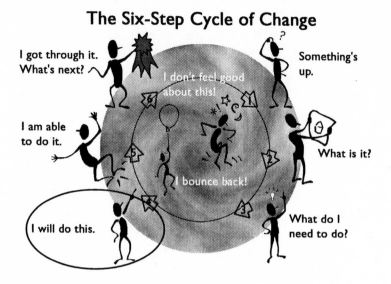

I got through it.
What's next?

Something's up.

I am able
to do it.

I don't feel good
about this!

What is it?

I bounce back!

I will do this.

What do I
need to do?

Step Four: I will do this!

When plans are made, they are put into action. Once you know what must be done, you do it.

Examples of Personal Change for Step Four

You know what to do, and now you do it. You shop for maternity clothes and buy furnishings for the nursery. You sign up for childbirth classes and begin attending.

Soon, however, you discover that no plan is perfect and correction is needed. You may find that you cannot actually afford an addition to your home, so a guest bedroom is converted into a nursery. You don't like your first choice of doctors, so you change.

Through daily working on your implementation plan, you are prepared for parenthood when the child is finally born.

Examples of Work Related Change for Step Four

Implementation plans are put into action.

◆ A support network is established.
◆ The new design is explained to employees.
◆ A target date is chosen and training is given.
◆ The system is led into reorganizing.

Unforeseen problems arise and revisions must be made to the plan; but with each adaptation success seems closer and a sense of competence begins to develop.

The Six-Step Cycle of Change

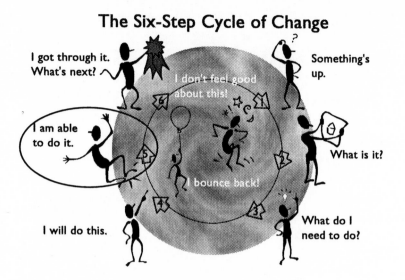

I got through it.
What's next?

Something's
up.

I don't feel good
about this!

I am able
to do it.

What is it?

I bounce back!

I will do this.

What do I
need to do?

Step Five: I am able to do it.

As the plan of action is used, it is modified and improved until there is a sense that it is working. The realization that the goal can be accomplished is slowly embraced and the change process continues toward the sixth step.

Examples of Personal Change for Step Five

As your plan of action is put into place, a series of adjustments will be needed. With enough experience and working through of problems, you discover that you are comfortable as a parent. Things are going more smoothly, and you find that you actually like getting up for intimate 3 a.m. feedings.

As you advance into this step on the cycle of change, you begin realizing that life is showing signs of a return to normalcy.

Examples of Work Related Change for Step Five:

With experience, the organization finds that it has made the needed changes and discovers that they are working. Unforeseen problems arise and adjustments continue to be made. Over time, the new procedures are proven successful.

Eventually there is a sense that, "We can do it." What seemed chaotic is becoming easier. Team spirit develops, and the beginning of a return to normalcy appears.

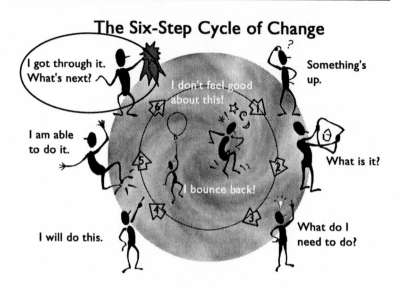

The Six-Step Cycle of Change

Step Six: I got through it. What is next?

As you approach the end of the change cycle, things settle back down to a routine and begin to feel normal. However, if you look ahead, you will sense that more change is on the horizon.

Examples of Personal Change for Step Six

Life has settled back down. You have weathered the change. Things are back to normal, but it is a new normal. You can now relax and enjoy family life with the baby, but look ahead on the cycle of change and you may get that familiar feeling that "Something's up." Normal does not last long, and soon you are off on a new round of change.

Examples of Work Related Change for Step Six

There is a return to normalcy of daily operations, but it is a new normal. In this new situation there is a carefully planned routine of scanning for the early indicators of the next change. By taking a proactive stance at this point, you are given an early warning of coming changes, which are surely on the way.

What about Sudden Change?

Change always follows this basic process, although it may sometimes bypass **Step One** and start at **Step Two**. Sudden change may come from an accident or an unexpected business reversal. With sudden change there is no sense that "Something's up," and while you cannot prepare in advance, the other steps in the change cycle remain the same.

As is typical of **Step Two**, you must first determine the nature of the situation confronting you. What has happened? What is the danger? What is the possibility? Once the issue can be stated, a plan of action must be formulated and put into place by following the remaining steps of the cycle. With experience and ongoing modification, a successful plan will return you to a state of normalcy.

The Center of the Change Cycle: Resistance and Resilience

At the heart of the change process are two key features: resistance and resilience. Whenever change enters our life, even if it is a desired change, it often has aspects that we do not like, and we naturally resist what we do not like.

Resistance is typically viewed as something negative because it can mobilize and direct energy toward blocking change. However, if resistance is accepted and understood in a positive way, its energy can be refocused into supporting the change process.

Confronting resistance requires resiliency, which is the ability to bounce back from challenge and adversity. Resiliency generates the positive energy needed to move forward in a meaningful and life-enhancing manner.

We will explore more about resistance and resiliency later. First, let's look at how the cycle of change works in daily life.

Using the Cycle of Change: Making Change Work for Us

We are surrounded by a multitude of changes. Sometimes we are being led into change. And, at other times, we instigate it. For many of us, work is where we are led into change; while in our homes, churches, and civic clubs, we may be the person initiating the change.

The cycle of change clearly indicates how to design change so that it is likely to succeed, and how it can be inadvertently designed to fail. A poorly led change has one easily recognizable feature: The change leader is out of sync with the people being led. Most often this becomes evident when a change initiative is announced and is perceived as a solution to a problem that people did not know existed.

Poorly Led Change at Home

Let's imagine an example of a poorly led change where you are the change agent. Suppose that in reading recent newspapers and magazines you have been noticing articles about the poor quality of the American diet and have become sensitized to the issue of "high fat content." One night, after watching an absorbing, television news report on nutritional needs, you are struck by the possibility that your family's diet may need overhauling. You sense that "Something's up."

Some quick investigation confirms that you are right. There is too much fat in the family meals, and you clearly state the newly seen problem: "We need a healthier diet."

Having identified the problem, you begin planning the solution. New food choices are required. On the next visit to the grocery store, you buy only low fat foods. You purchase several soybean and grain meat substitute products and also return home with many new and exotic fruits and vegetables. Having acquired the food, you implement your solution by preparing it for the very next evening meal; and when your family comes to the table, they are greeted with an array of "never before seen" dishes.

Poking and prodding through the assortment, they hesitantly ask, "What is this?" When you inform them that it is their new low fat diet, much resistance is evident as they proclaim, "We didn't ask for this, and we don't want it." Your desired change has stalled because you offered your family a solution to a problem that they did not know they had.

On the cycle of change you were too far ahead of them. Change is destined to go poorly when the change leader is out of sync with those being led into change. For change to have a better chance of success, everyone needs to understand the problem before the solution is presented. The change leader's task is to sell the problem and not the solution. If people understand the problem, they will seek a solution.

To be successful in changing your family's diet, try gathering them at **Step Two** of the change cycle. Even better, try to get them to recognize the signs of a need to change, so they can help formulate and clarify the issue.

When you begin noticing those newspaper articles on the poor American diet, pass them along to others. Ask if they have seen similar information at school or work (**Step One**). At a family meeting you could discuss the information gathered. As a group, you can decide whether or not your family's diet has too much fat (**Step Two**) and, if the answer is yes, make plans for a change (**Step Three**).

When the plan is complete, your family goes shopping together, and everyone chooses healthier food that they would like to try. Next, everyone participates in the preparation of the meal (**Step Four**) and when it is placed on the table there is a much better chance of successful change. As a group, the family has moved around the cycle of change and learns that change can work (**Step Five**). Soon they are headed toward a new normalcy in dietary habits (**Step Six**) and are already looking for further change to come along.

Leading Change at Work

In many work settings, change is typically initiated at **Step Four**. Perhaps you have come to work and been told of a new change which was essentially a solution to a problem that you did not know you had.

Such changes are hard to accept because you do not understand the reasons for them. Also, you may quickly spot some very real problems with the proposed change. From your front line position, you may immediately know of several reasons why the suggested change will not work, but your input into the planning was not solicited.

In these instances of poorly initiated change, what has most likely happened is that one person observed some random incidents and sensed "Something's up." Having identified a problem, plans were made for what needed to be done. Once the plan was complete, it was announced to you and your co-workers who, unfortunately, had not yet even sensed that anything was awry. In the absence of an identified problem, the change makes no sense. (If it's not broke, don't fix it.) Had you been informed of a problem and asked to help clarify it, your ideas may have been critical in designing a workable solution.

The key point to leading effective change is this. You must gather people at the stage of clarification—**Step Two**—before advancing to solutions.

Following the Change Cycle

Change works best when the change cycle is rigorously followed. In the ideal work situation everyone in the organization is trained to scan a wide variety of areas for random incidents of coming change. This information is frequently shared and discussed by many people so that there can be an early identification and consensus regarding problems and opportunities.

Once the situation can be clearly stated, action planning begins and utilizes diverse work teams including all levels of personnel to determine what needs to happen, how it needs to be done, and when it is to start. This approach to managing change ensures all levels of the issue can be addressed. When such a well-developed plan is implemented, there is general support for it because many workers understand the reasons for change and actually had a hand in the planning process.

With encouragement and rewards for identifying unforeseen problems of implementation, employees will give feedback that should be well received and positively acted upon so necessary adjustments to the plan can be made. Over time the sense that "we can do it" develops, and eventually there is a return to a state of normal operations where once again the scanning for signs of coming change occurs.

The Emotional Model of Change

The six-step Cycle of Change we have been exploring is a cognitive model of how the process of change works. It explains the steps of change and the tasks that are required at each step. While the presence of resistance and resiliency highlights some of the negative and positive reactions to change, the full range of emotions has not been presented. Change brings specific and predictable emotional responses, and in order to facilitate change, it is important to understand what they are. A helpful model for understanding the emotions of change comes from the Middle Ages with the image of the Wheel of Life.

The Wheel of Life is the medieval model of change, and it describes the phases and emotions of the change process. At a time when many people were illiterate, teaching took place through images or pictures. The visual lessons of the Wheel of Life were so important that it was often carved into the stone of the walls of cathedrals for all to see. People viewing the image were receiving instructions about the nature of change. What were the lessons?

At the top of the Wheel of Life we see a smiling, well-dressed individual who could be a person of nobility. This individual is in the position of Happiness. Life is normal and things are going well. When change occurs, however, the wheel turns with a clockwise movement. The same person, now with a look of distress, is upside down and falling through space. This is the position of Loss. As the wheel continues its movement, we find, at the bottom of the wheel, an individual who is now nude and is being pulled through the hard times of life. This is the position of Suffering. The wheel turns once more, and the individual, again clothed, rises up to the position of Hope. From Hope there is anticipation of returning to the state of Happiness. The fundamental lesson of the Wheel of Life is that these four positions of happiness, loss, suffering, and hope are our only options in life, and we are always in the midst of one of them or moving on to the next.

Happiness is where everything seems normal. Happy is where we all want to be. It is here that whatever we are doing is succeeding. Life is smooth and comfortable because we have an established routine that works.

Loss is where happiness begins to fall apart. We have glimpsed the signal of coming change and are challenged to let go of what we have worked to create. When loss comes, we want to return to happiness as quickly as possible. We wish we could regain our equilibrium by making the wheel go in reverse. The wheel, however, only moves forward with a clockwise movement. To regain happiness, we must follow it into Suffering.

Suffering lies at the bottom of the wheel and represents the process of transition. The Latin root word for suffering means "to experience" or "to allow." To suffer in this sense means that we must go through and fully experience our loss, so we can make, and then implement, plans for a return to normalcy. If we want to return to happiness, the process of suffering cannot be short-circuited. We cannot go over, under, or around this difficult phase of transition. We must go through it with the hard work of becoming conscious of our responsibility and choices. In the phase of suffering, we must devise an effective coping strategy for changing. This process is often unpleasant because it brings the accompanying normal, but distressing, emotions of tension, anxiety, worry, frustration, anger, conflict, and sadness. It is out of the suffering and "living-through" experience of the Wheel that Hope emerges.

Hope returns only when our plan and our efforts at coping are succeeding and some progress is made. As the reality of achieving our goal comes into view, we begin to feel a sense of competence, and we have a vision of the return to Happiness. The normalcy that we find, however, will not be the same as the "old normal." Through an effective process of change we return to balance, but it is a new and different balance. Happiness is found again, but in a new and different state of equilibrium.

Once back to normal, if we look ahead, the uneasy sense that change is coming again appears on the horizon. The winds of change are always blowing. The Wheel of Life always turns. Happiness is not a permanent state. More change will come, and the journey around the wheel into loss, suffering, and hope begins again. This is the normal life process of growth toward increasing levels of maturity.

Whenever change enters our life, we experience the emotions of change. As we sense that Loss is coming, there is anxiety, apprehension, and worry. When Loss arrives we feel sad, angry, irritated, and frustrated. Grieving needs to be done. With the experience of the living-through or suffering of change may come stress, depression, burnout, helplessness, or even hopelessness. Eventually, Hope arises and brings a renewal of energy, optimism, and enthusiasm while the return to Happiness brings a sense of satisfaction, accomplishment, and contentment.

The Wheel of Life teaches that we cannot get happy and stay happy. If we did, we would not know that we were happy after a week. Reaching the top of the Wheel and staying there would mean that we were in a state of being in which things were the same day after day. We have a word for this: boredom. The only

way that you can know you are happy today is to have
been unhappy yesterday. You must have a point of
comparison. It is the turning of the Wheel and the ups
and downs of life that guard against complacency and
offer to enrich our experience. To obtain such enrich-
ment, however, we must be willing to enter Loss and
Suffering.

Most people do not want to do this, and our culture
does not support it because in America we are guaran-
teed the right to the pursuit of happiness. Our pursuit
often takes the form of the denial and avoidance of the
difficulties of change and of life. We try to pretend that
nothing is wrong. We attempt to skip over the "living
through experience" that is in reality the transforma-
tion experience. Avoiding the full acceptance of change
only means that you get to experience the change over
and over until you learn the lesson.

Change is always occurring and bringing with it the
possibility of growth. The different phases and emotions of change are expected and normal. They cannot
be avoided. Look for and accept them in yourself and
others, and you will be better able to work through the
recurrent process of change. If you know the emotions
of change, then you know what to expect in yourself
and others.

Multiple Cycles of Change

Assess your life and you will most likely find that you
are traveling in several different cycles of change at
once. You have one cycle at work, and when you are at

home, there is another. Church, community, and world changes all add to the number and complexity of change cycles, and these cycles are not well synchronized. You go through Loss in one area of your life, as you begin to regain Hope in another. In some instances you are being led into change while in others you are doing the leading.

Emotionally, there are also a variety of experiences. There are many different emotional wheels of life, and they keep turning through all four phases. Learning to balance the evolving, emotional intricacy of change is where the real challenge of managing change is found. It is here at the heart of change that the real work must be done.

The Heart of Change:
Resistance and Resiliency

A t the heart of the change process are found the two key features of resistance and resiliency. Whenever any change enters our lives, there are aspects of it that we do not like. Resistance arises and it can mobilize energy directed at blocking change. However, if resistance is properly understood and accepted, its energy can be refocused into supporting change.

Resiliency refers to an ability to bounce back from challenge and adversity. It enables a quick recovery from misfortune and is a helpful attribute to have when confronting change. If you are to survive and thrive when confronting the challenges of changing, you need to understand resistance and to possess the skills of resiliency. Let's explore resistance and then look at resiliency.

Understanding Resistance

At the center of the change cycle we find resistance. Resistance to change is normal and always happens. It shows up whenever we confront something new and think to ourselves, "I don't like it."

In the field of electronics the concept of resistance is well understood. It can be defined as the opposition of a body or substance to an electric current passing through it and resulting in a change of electrical energy into heat or another form of energy. The heat or other by-products are often desired and useful but can also create problems.

A modification of this definition to apply to people and the change process would state, "Resistance is the opposition of people to change passing through them, resulting in energy, which can transform or stop progress." With this definition the most important aspect of resistance is that it brings energy that is valuable because it can be capitalized upon to facilitate the change process. However, in order to productively utilize resistance, we must learn to embrace it rather than to avoid it. We must come to understand that resistance is fundamentally just a source of information and can be very useful.

Human beings are naturally resistant to change. Survival of our species has depended upon being able to quickly scan the environment for any change that signaled potential danger, so it could be avoided if possible. As a consequence, we are fundamentally danger oriented and when anything new arises in the environment, we quickly look to see how it might present a risk. When it is perceived as threatening, we avoid or resist it. This is a useful response because when we encounter a new change we need to always assess its possible danger. Resistance can help keep us safe, but it may also bring progress to a halt if it blocks our seeking to find the opportunity that may also be present in change. We must learn to look for the deeper, positive, and often hidden message of resistance.

Resisting Yourself

In case you doubt that resistance is natural, consider how you actually resist your own self-initiated changes. Most likely, you have worked hard to bring about a change in your life that you sincerely wanted, but then immediately resisted when the opportunity to change presented itself.

Can you think of such a time? For example, have you ever decided to lose weight by planning a diet or an exercise program? If so, you may recall that you resisted your efforts at change. On the first day of your diet what did you do? Either you broke the diet right away, or you decided to start "next week." This is resistance.

In regard to your plan for exercise, you might decide to awaken each morning at 5:30 a.m. and go on a 30-minute run. What happens the next morning when the alarm sounds? That's right, you hit the snooze alarm and go back to sleep. For several days in a row you do the same thing. You are busy resisting change.

A central point to recognize about your resistance is that it is trying to tell you something. Resistance is information, and we must actively seek to understand the message, or we will derail the change we are trying to make.

What do you think that turning off the alarm is trying to tell you? Most likely, the message is not that you should not exercise. If you looked into the mirror and decided that you needed to lose weight, you are probably right. Your resistance to getting out of bed so early may be simply saying that this is a bad plan for you. You may not be a morning exercise person. Your resistance is telling you to change the plan. Try switching to 5:30 p.m., and it may work fine. You are an afternoon exercise person; not a morning person.

It is the same with dieting. Your resistance to dieting does not mean you should not lose weight. It most likely means that the diet you are trying is not right for you. It may be too stringent or inappropriate in some other way. Change the type of diet and things may go fine.

Resistance is information. Learning to listen to the resistance and to understand its message will help you make the changes in life that you need. The same is true with organizational changes.

Resisting Others

If you resist your own planned changes, guess what happens when someone else offers you a change?

Resistance once again arises and may be much more intense than when you resist yourself.

We often resist the changes that other people offer us because we did not expect them. When someone provides us with the solution to a problem that we did not know we had, we are caught off guard and not prepared. We become resistant because we do not understand why change is needed.

In this instance, what has occurred is that the change leader is at the implementation stage of the change cycle (**Step Four**), while we do not even have an idea that "Something's up" (**Step One**). We need to be brought up to speed, and we need to have the freedom to ask for necessary background information. The leader of the change process must be open to such questioning because once the reasons for change are understood, we may be more cooperative and supportive of it.

If the change leader is too far ahead in the cycle of change, resistance may arise even when we understand the reasons for change. What happens is that when the change is presented, you immediately see several good reasons why it will not work as planned. Here, the fundamental problem is that you were not included in the planning process (**Step Three**), and those who planned it did not see it from your unique perspective. Upper management may have created the plan with limited input from front line staff; however, as a front line staff person (who is intimately familiar with daily operations) you spot several major obstacles that must be overcome. You resist the change because you know that, in the long run, it will not work. For the change to succeed you must be able to voice your concerns so that adjustments can be made and the process improved.

You will risk voicing your concerns only if you believe that your "resistance" is valued. Traditionally, resistance has been seen as negative and people who resisted were thought of as being "bad" for the organization. Resistance was something to be squelched so that progress could go on. However, what usually happened is that the resistance went underground where it could grow out of control.

We now understand that most resistance is helpful because it is trying to tell us something we need to know. In addition, resistance always brings energy, which it may be possible to mobilize in support of the change. This will only happen, however, if the leaders of change process are able to engage resistance. To engage resistance you must first be able to recognize and acknowledge it.

Recognizing Resistance

We all resist change, and we have our favorite ways of doing so. Do you know what your favorite techniques of resistance are? Here is how to find out.

Imagine that you are at the dinner table and your spouse or significant other says to you, "We need to talk." Is this good news? Are you pleased and do you say something like, "It's about time. I thought you would never get around to it." Most likely, anxiety arises as you can feel your stomach knotting up. You begin thinking, "What is this all about? How can I get out of it?"

You might try one of several strategies of resistance. You could use avoidance by clearing the dinner dishes, leaving the table to go to the sink, and not returning. Diversion might work, if you change the subject quickly enough. Suspecting that a fight is coming, you could try a counter offensive move and start an argument about a topic on which you are sure you could win.

Whatever you do in an effort at avoidance will be one of your ways of resisting. Your first impulse is likely to be your typical way of resisting.

Resistance appears in common patterns. When change is announced in an organization, you may see indications of anger, irritation, and frustration. People may appear confused and not able to understand what they are being told. Quick criticism ranging from mild to intense will appear. There may be attempts to sabotage the change process. People may too easily agree with what they do not fully comprehend. There may be wholesale denial that any change will ever happen. Malicious compliance to every small detail may kill the process. Absenteeism may occur as workers call in "sick." All of these reactions signal resistance.

One of the most common indicators of resistance occurs when a planned change is announced to a group, and there is a call for questions. As the change leader you might ask, "Well, what do you think?" Usually there is a long, "loud" silence. No one has any thing to say. If you are naive about the process of change, you think to yourself, "This is great. It is going to be easier that I thought." Silence, however, almost always means there is strong resistance in a situation where no one feels safe enough to voice it. Unspoken resistance goes underground where it grows and becomes stronger.

Responses to Resistance

Change leaders are at risk for colluding with resistance by not seeking it out. This happens because, in addition to our usual ways of resisting, we also have typical responses to resistance. If you do not seek out resistance and bring it into awareness, then you are in effect working against the change that you are trying to bring about.

What are the typical or default responses to perceived resistance?

One common response is to ignore it. For example, you do not explore the long silence after a call for questions and hope that whatever it represents will just go away. Other non-helpful responses to resistance are:

◆   Using power: Try to make people go along.
◆   Using reason: Explain it once again in more detail.
◆   Manipulating: Play one person against another and maybe it will work.

◆ Using relationships: Call in favors owed to you.
◆ Making deals: Compromise and dilute the change.
◆ Giving up too soon: Lose motivation and quit.

These well-worn reactions to resistance view it as something negative that is to be avoided or controlled. To overcome such typical reactions, you must see resistance in a different light. You must understand resistance as potentially helpful because it brings needed information and energy. Just as your resistance to personal change (weight loss and exercise) brought information, so too does the resistance encountered in families and organizations.

Embracing Resistance

In order to find out what information is hidden in resistance, you must learn to move towards and embrace resistance. Just accept that resistance is always present, and seek it out.

The uncovering of resistance must be done in the context of strong working relationships that can sustain some give-and-take. If such relationships do not exist, then they must be built. With strong relationships, a clear focus on the goals of the change, and the openness for discussion, resistance can be embraced and brought to light.

Furthermore, it is critical to maintain respect for people who resist change. The best working assumption is that these people know something valuable that you do not. They see the proposed change from a different perspective and can identify problematic issues. People who resist and are willing to take the risk of confronting you with their resistance are valuable assets. If their objections can be integrated into the plan for change, it will not only improve the plan but will mobilize their energy in support of the process.

When there is resistance to change, people are usually divided into different factions all asking the same narrowly focused question, "What is in it for me?" Embracing the resistance of these differing groups is an attempt to change the nature of this question so that all parties are asking, "What is in it for us?" This is the question that will bring people together while also mobilizing energy for change.

Resistance and the Cycle of Change

Resistance can have a significant negative impact at each of the six steps of the Cycle of Change. At **Step One** of "Something's up" you simply do not look ahead or ask any question about what is going on. At **Step Two** you refuse to name or even give the slightest acknowledgement to any problem. Refusing to make any plans for action will stall you at **Step Three,** as will never acting on plans you did make when you reach **Step Four.** You can resist at **Step Five** by never making any adjustments to plans that are implemented. At **Step Six,** complacency will lull you into false security, and you will not proactively look ahead to what is coming.

The Six-Step Cycle of Change

I got through it. What's next?
Be complacent!

Something's up.
Don't look ahead!

I am able to do it.
Don't adjust!

Resistance

What is it?
Don't name it!

I will do this.
Don't begin!

What do I need to do?
Don't plan!

Understanding Resiliency

Coping with the ongoing tumult of change, requires resiliency because it is resiliency that provides the strength needed to confront resistance and to do the difficult work of repeatedly engaging the Cycle of Change. Resiliency not only enables us to bounce back from the ups and downs of life, but also provides the energy to move forward in solving life problems, confronting challenges, and overcoming obstacles. While most people are naturally resilient, resiliency must be nurtured, or it will be lost. We have a limited supply of resiliency energy, and it must be replenished as it is used up.

To better understand your resiliency resources, picture (in your mind's eye) a functional reservoir system with the water of a lake held behind a dam. Think of the water as representing all of the energy you have to put into life. As daily changes and stresses are encountered, the floodgates of the dam open and some of the water/energy is drained away to help you cope with the challenges you face.

Minor changes drain away a small amount of the water. Bigger changes drain away more; and a rapid series of unanticipated changes or a major traumatic event can open the floodgates so wide that the lake will run dry. With resiliency resources depleted, no energy is left for life, and you experience the symptoms of "burnout" or depression, in which motivation is lost and everything appears dull and dreary. To avoid such a desperate situation, you must know how to replenish the energy of life as it is used up.

Assessing Your Resiliency Resources

◆   How do you keep your energy level up?
◆   What are you doing to take care of yourself?

If you are to maintain resiliency, these are the essential questions that must be answered.

Try this simple exercise to assess your resiliency resources. Get a blank sheet of paper and number from 1-20 down the left-hand side. Now, quickly make a list of 20 things that you like to do. You can list anything at all. The order is not important, and an item does not have to be something that you are currently doing. If you have ever enjoyed it, you can add it to your list.

As you do this exercise, pay close attention to what happens. You might notice something unusual. Many people do. You may be surprised to find that this is hard work. You may be even more surprised to find that you begin to run out of items around number 10. This is a typical, but rather frustrating and ultimately sad, response.

It becomes especially distressing when you stop to consider all of life's possibilities for enjoyment. How many options are available? There may be hundreds of thousands or perhaps millions. Let's suppose that there are a million possibilities for fun, and you can't even think of 20 of them. Now, can you see why this is sad? With a short list of options for enjoyment, you have a very restricted repertoire for sustaining your resiliency.

Having just a few choices gives you a limited menu for
fun. It is like going to a restaurant when you are very
hungry, only to discover that there are just three items
on the menu, and realizing that you can't stand any of
them. You will have to either eat something you do not
like or do without. Meager choices for fun are restrict-
ing in the way that a list containing no indoor activities limits the enjoyment of a rainy day. With limited
choices for enjoying life, you will have difficulty keeping your resiliency level up. To ensure resiliency, you
must increase your options. How can you add to your
list?

One way is to get another person to make their own
list of what they like to do and then compare. In so
doing, each person will be reminded of things they like
to do but had forgotten, and these can be added to the
list of resiliency activities. Try this with several people
and the list of enjoyable activities will continue to
grow.

In addition, you might consider the fact that there are
two basic categories of things to enjoy. One consists of
those things that you like to do because they are fun,
and the other category concerns those things you like
because they give you a sense of accomplishment
when you do them. What do you have on your list? Is
it mostly fun items? Did you forget accomplishments?

Think of washing the dishes. This activity can be very
satisfying because you can clearly see that something
was accomplished. You start with dirty dishes and fin-
ish with clean ones. On some days this may be the

only time you get such clear-cut results. Other examples might be cleaning a closet, cooking a meal, or cutting the grass. Hopefully, going to work and doing your job are included. A job well done can be very satisfying. Be sure that your list of things you like to do includes items from both categories of fun and accomplishment.

Once you have a list of 20 things you like to do, you must determine if it is actually helping you by giving your list a test. To do this, read over your list and put the letter "W" by each item that you actually did in the past week. The number of things you have enjoyed will influence your current mood.

If you did about 75% of the items on your list, you will probably report a great week. Even 50% could make a good week. Less than 50% and you may be in trouble. If you have only done about 25% of the items on your list, life may be looking rather unpleasant, and if you have done nothing that you like in the past week then life probably looks grim.

Burnout: Lack of Resiliency

If you find that you did nothing in the past week that was enjoyable, you may be noticing some of the symptoms of burnout. These symptoms are very similar to those of depression and include reports of a lack of energy and motivation. Your mood may be one of sadness, and you may be showing increasing levels of irritation and frustration. Burnout is what happens when resiliency resources run low. (You will find a burnout inventory on page 88 of this book or you can take the test online at www.lessonsforliving.com.)

When you are depressed or burned out, you may withdraw from others in an attempt to regroup your resources. If someone comes along at this time and invites you to do one of your favorite activities from your list of things you enjoy, you will most likely have the same standard answer to give. You first say, "No" and then give a reason. Most often the reason is, "I don't feel like it."

With this answer you are concisely summing up your philosophy of life. You are saying that in life you should not do things until you feel like doing so. Your intention is one of waiting, but for what? Until you "feel like it?" If so, consider this question, "How long will it take you to feel like it?" The answer is of course unknown. You might feel like it in a few minutes and go running after the person who invited you, or it may take you days, weeks, or months "to feel like it."

At this point in time your basic life strategy can be described as one of "waiting for a miracle." You are waiting to be zapped by something from outside of yourself that will fill you with motivation, ambition, interest, and energy and make you want to do "it" (whatever "it" is) without you having to do a single thing. Furthermore, you don't intend to move until this happens. Waiting for such a miracle is not the best plan for life. You must learn how to make the miracle for yourself.

Making a Miracle

Consider this question. What comes first in life, action or motivation? The usual answer given is motivation, but luckily for us the correct answer is action. If you are motivated, that is well and good, but if not, you can create motivation through action.

Perhaps you have had this experience. Someone wants you to go somewhere that you don't want to go. It may be to a movie, party, or family reunion. You say, "No. I don't feel like it." But, they keep asking and pressuring until, with great reluctance and only after secretly vowing to make them miserable, you agree to go. Once arriving at your destination, however, it only takes a few minutes to start having a great time. In fact, the experience proves to be one of the best times of your life.

Now, what was your motivation for going? None. It was zero. But, you acted anyway and placed yourself in the circumstances where motivation could catch up with you. It is important to understand that action can precede motivation. And, whether we feel like it or not, we can make ourselves act, thereby, taking control of creating our motivation. When we do so, we add to our levels of enjoyment and resiliency.

Taking action is especially important with the things you already like to do. If you have ever enjoyed an activity, you most likely would enjoy doing it again. Act first and the motivation will follow. Intentionally, do one of your enjoyable activities, whether you feel like it or not, and chances are that you will enjoy it. With this sense of enjoyment your energy will rise, and consequently, you will now "feel like" doing more things. As you continue to act and create motivation, your level of resiliency rises, and you replenish your reservoir of life energy. As resiliency increases, symptoms of burnout begin to lessen.

The paradoxical secret of being a resilient person is this. Everyday you have to do something you "enjoy," whether or not you feel like doing so. In other words, have fun, whether you feel like it or not. How you feel is not as important as what you do. Don't wait until you feel like it. Do it anyway.

A practical example of this process is physical exercise. Many people who exercise regularly find that there are some days when they do not want to do it. They don't feel like running, swimming, or going to aerobics class. Once they begin the activity, however, their interest builds, and they are more energized at the end. Action leads to motivation, which creates a sense of enjoyment that builds more motivation.

Planning for Fun

Return again to your list of things you like to do. We have taken a look at how often you engage in these activities, but there are other factors to consider in determining how useful this list is to you. For example, how much planning does it take you to enjoy something?

Read each item on your list again and put the letter "P" by each one that takes more than 15 minutes of just getting ready do it. We are trying to find out how quickly you can do something that will build up your resiliency level. If you like to go to the movies, but have to drive 30 minutes in traffic to get to the theater, this requires planning and a "P."

Items that require planning and organization, such as that trip to Europe, the long awaited concert, or the upcoming family reunion, are important. These items build anticipation which, in itself, is enjoyable and can pull you along through hard times. However, if most of your items have a "P" by them, then you require significant levels of structure and organization in order to have fun. You may lack spontaneity. To be fully resilient, you also need some items that take no planning because these activities enable you to quickly build up your energy reserves. What kind of things can you quickly do? How about:

◆ Taking a walk
◆ Listening to music
◆ Calling a friend
◆ Reading a book
◆ Petting your dog
◆ Having a cup of coffee

These are simple pleasures that take little effort or planning, but, when fully appreciated, can lift your spirits very quickly. Fully appreciating an activity means being present to the moment and not distracting yourself with multitasking activities. When you are petting your dog, just pet your dog. Don't try to do something else at the same time. Give your full attention to just one activity. Remember, building and maintaining your resiliency resources requires a creative mixture of spontaneous and planned activities.

The Cost of Resiliency

Another way of assessing your ability to enjoy life is to see how much money it costs you to have fun?

Reread all the items on your list, and this time put a dollar sign ($) by each item that costs you more than $10.00 each time you do it. When you are through, if everything has a $ by it, then you had best have lots of money, or you will be having no fun.

Ideally, you need a balance between items that cost and those that are free. Free items help you enjoy life even when you have no money to spend, but investing your money into certain activities, like a vacation to an exotic location, brings you a special experience. You need both categories. Try to develop a balanced list.

Resiliency for One

One final way to evaluate your list of things you like to do is to place the letter "A" by each item that you usually do alone. If you find that you do very few things you enjoy alone, it may be that you depend too much on others to entertain you and create enjoyment for you. If you do everything alone, you may be isolating yourself from others and robbing yourself of the enjoyment of relationships. Again, you are looking for a balance on your list. Try to add the items that you need to bring more of a balance to your life.

Having a list of things that you enjoy is a quick way of assessing your capacity and ability to develop and maintain your resiliency level. The more you utilize your choices to have fun or accomplish something that is meaningful to you; the more resilient you will become.

The Box of Life

Another way of looking at the issue of resiliency is to imagine life as a box.

Work

Picture the Box of Life and decide what fills it up. Some people have the strategy of filling the box with just one thing. For example, some people fill the Box of Life with work. They tend to look at life through the window of work. When work is going well, life looks good. However, if there is a bad day at work, life begins to look frustrating and depressing. For other people the Box of Life is filled with the "one thing" of a relationship. When the relationship is good, life is good. When the relationship is struggling, life seems negative. Filling the Box of Life with just one thing is not a good strategy.

Ideally, the Box of Life is divided into many small compartments and each is filled with something meaningful, fun, or creative. Your Box of Life may be filled with work, family, church, hobbies, pets, reading, exercise, and so on. On a day when work is not good, you still have other windows through which to view life. Work may represent only one-twelfth of life, and when that is not good, the other eleven-twelfths may be fine. With a Box of Life filled with variety, you have many choices to revitalize yourself. Invest your energy into each area every day and your resiliency will be high. You will more easily bounce back from adversity because of your many readily available resources.

Work	Friends	Exercise	School
Fishing	Family	Church	Garden
Hobby	Charity	Pets	Music

The Importance of Attitude

U ltimately, whether or not you choose to practice the skills of becoming a resilient person will depend upon your attitude. In determining how we face life, it is our attitude that is the key. To understand the importance of attitude, consider the following statement. Is it true or false?

You are responsible for all of your experiences of life.

The correct answer is "true." You are always responsible for your experiences of life. However, the statement is somewhat of a trick. Notice that it does not say "experiences in life" but "experiences of life." You are not responsible for everything that happens to you, but you are responsible for how you react to what does happen to you.

Your reaction to life events is always under your control. In any life situation you are invariably responsible for at least one thing. You are always responsible for the attitude you adopt toward the situation in which you find yourself. Your attitude determines your reaction to what life hands you; and attitudes can be positive or negative. Fortunately, even the worst attitude can be changed; and with the right attitude, you can become a more resilient person.

What is an attitude? It is simply a point of view about a situation. It is an outlook on life. An attitude has three components.

- What you think.
- What you do.
- What you feel.

No matter in what situation you find yourself, you always have thoughts about it. You make a judgment as to its goodness or badness for you. You also have an emotional response to your judgment. You could be happy, sad, or angry. Furthermore, your behavior takes a certain form. You may be laughing, crying, or punching the wall.

If you want to change an attitude, you either change your thinking, change the way you act, or change the way you feel. Of these three options, changing your thinking and behavior is easier than changing your emotions.

Unfortunately, when we have a negative attitude, our initial tendency is to focus on the feeling level and to try and change it first. The feeling or emotional level, however, is the most difficult one to work on because you can't readily "grasp" a feeling and force it to change. Feelings are powerful, but vague. Nonetheless, when we feel sad, angry, anxious, or frustrated, we usually want the feeling to go away and to do so quickly. So, we begin the process by trying to change our emotions. This effort can take a variety of forms.

We often begin by trying to change other people so we can feel better. We think that if we can make others be the way that we want them to be, then it will lessen our distress. However, it hardly ever works. So, we may engage in behaviors like alcohol and drug use hoping to numb the feelings. Further attempts at avoiding emotional distress are seen in becoming either a workaholic or a non-stop shopper. None of these efforts succeed.

If you want to change your feelings, you must start elsewhere. You must begin where you have more control by recognizing that it is easier to influence the way you think or behave than to change your emotions.

The secret to effectively changing emotions is in knowing that feelings, thoughts, and behaviors are all interconnected. When you change one of them (for example, thinking) the other two (feelings and behavior) will change as well. Since it is easier to get a "grasp" on thoughts and behavior than on feelings, this is the place to begin your work of becoming and staying resilient. Change what you think, or change what you do, and your emotions will follow suit. Do so and you will be creating resiliency for yourself.

You Are What You Think

Change your thinking and life will get better. But, how do you know which thoughts to change? Your troublesome thoughts, the ones that increase your misery over a situation, can easily be found in your inner self-talk, which is that private running dialogue you have with yourself.

We all have an inner voice that speaks to us. You might think of it as the Voice of Conscience. It appears as that "inner observer" who always seems to be sitting in the corner and watching everything you do. You may recognize it as that Voice that starts talking to you when you wake up in the morning. Sometimes it may wait until you get out of bed, wander into the bathroom, and look in the mirror before it actually speaks. It is that Voice that says, "You are so slim, and your hair looks beautiful." Or, "You sure are handsome." Perhaps, it says, "You are going to have a great day." It might muse, "What a wonderful person you are."

If you don't recognize this positive Voice, then yours may be speaking to you in a different tone. Sometimes it seems that the Voice of Conscience is in a bad mood. You might be hearing, "You look terrible." Or, "You sure have gained a lot of weight, and your hair is a mess." You may hear, "It's going to be a bad day! Stay in bed. Don't get up."

This Voice (the negative, critical voice that is full of exaggeration) is one of the main reasons people have so many problems. It can easily destroy reserves of resiliency by opening the floodgates to our resiliency resources and draining away our energy.

A negative Voice of Conscience can make anything worse. For example, if you are like most people, you probably know how to take any small problem, think about it for a while, and turn it into a big problem. All it takes is for your inner voice to point out all of the dark possibilities and keep reminding you what might go wrong. Your imagination creates an increasingly unpleasant scenario, which you begin to believe. The problem escalates from a mild annoyance to a major catastrophe as you convince yourself that the imagined situation is the real situation. You become preoccupied with confronting a major problem that may only exist in your mind.

At this point, any response you make is going to be out of proportion to the real event. A realistic reaction to the original situation may have been a mild degree of emotional distress. So, if you were laid off from a job, you should be feeling some combination of worry, anxiety, sadness, irritation, frustration, or anger. All of these are normal and expected emotions for such an experience.

However, your inner Voice may be busy exaggerating with a dialogue such as, "This is horrible. It's the world's worst thing. No one will ever hire you. You'll never find another job, and you won't be able to pay your bills. You'll lose everything. You should just give up. It's hopeless."

With such a negative running commentary, you will soon either fall into depression or become enraged at your imagined mistreatment. In the depths of depression you may decide that the situation is hopeless, as you withdraw and isolate yourself from others. Or, in a state of rage, you may act in an inappropriate, violent manner towards your former employer. Either reaction is too intense because it is a response is to a situation you have created in your mind.

Change your mind—your attitude—and the problem can shrink back to its original size. The original problem may be bad enough, but it is not the catastrophe you have invented.

To change your attitude, you must change the inner dialogue. To change the dialogue, you must catch it in action. To do this you have to pay attention to your thinking. You must engage in self-observation and listen for what your inner voice is saying.

You can practice in this manner. The next time that you find yourself feeling "bad," don't immediately start asking, "Who did this to me?" Don't start looking around for the external cause of your problems. The thing to do is to ask, "What have I been thinking? What have I been telling myself?" Make the effort to discover how your inner dialogue has created your emotional distress.

Rules for Living

Our inner Voice of Conscience is based on underlying assumptions about how life should be. Every society has rules to help us interpret our experience. These rules explain the way things are. Some of the rules help create and maintain resiliency, while other rules hinder the process.

Here is a common rule that many of us learned. Our parents and teachers often emphasized it. *Whenever you do anything, do it right.* With this rule we try to be perfect and adopt a belief that, "Mistakes are bad."

Consequently, we work hard not to make any mistakes because if we do, it may mean that we too are somehow flawed or bad.

Assume that you firmly believe that mistakes are bad and have begun working on a project that is something you have never done before. Perhaps, it is building a table, baking a cake, or completing a new work assignment. Initially, you are excited, but soon something goes wrong. Somewhere along the way a mistake was made. When the mistake is discovered, your inner Voice speaks up, and you hear something like, "Well, look at this. You really messed up. You can't do anything right. You are so stupid! Why do you even bother to try? You should just give up." Soon your mood plummets, and you are feeling miserable, angry, or frustrated and are ready to quit.

If someone comes along, finds you in despair, and asks what is wrong, you might say, "Well look at that table I was making. See how it wobbles. It is all wrong." With this statement you are in essence claiming that the table is responsible for your mood.

However, what has actually brought about your distress? Was it the mistake you made (the wobbly table) or was it your reaction to the mistake? The answer is that it was your reaction in the form of all the negative inner dialogue in which you engaged. It is your inner criticism that has upset you.

The truth is that a mistake is just a normal life event with many possible reactions. Your specific reaction depends upon what you think mistakes mean, and what you think they mean depends on your rule for mistakes. If your rule is that mistakes are bad, then when you make one, you may decide that it means that you too are "bad." Many of us learned that a mistake is sign of failure, and this belief can lead to self-criticism. However, such a rule is just one of many. There are other points of view about what a mistake is.

When my daughter was six years old and trying to learn to ride a bicycle, she taught me a different rule. After falling off the bike many times, as you do with this learning process, she observed, "When you learn to ride a bicycle, you have to start with the falling down." I thought, "How insightful and how true." We learn by making mistakes. Fall off the bike and get back up enough times and you learn to ride.

So, a good rule for mistakes is, "A mistake is the first step in learning." Whenever you try to learn something new, progress comes from making a mistake and correcting it. If you make no mistakes, you don't learn. Whenever I go snow skiing and take a lesson, the instructor usually reminds me, "If you are not falling, you are not learning."

So mistakes are not bad; they are good. They help us learn. Adopt this rule and the next time you make a mistake, you should become excited as you say to yourself, "This is great. I'm going to learn something now!" It may be that in order to learn quickly, you should make as many mistakes as you to maximize your opportunities. Of course, this assumes that it is not the same mistake over and over again.

You can try this *rethinking* approach with any problem and see if both your mood and behavior improve.

Once, my wife was making a cake for our daughter to take to a school bake sale. She does not enjoy baking but was willing to make the effort. After several hours, however, when the cake was removed from the oven and the icing was applied, it began splitting down the middle with a large crack. The cake was declared to be "ruined." As it was late in the evening, it was too late to start over or to go to the store and buy a "real" cake.

My wife's inner dialogue was stated loud and clear, "This is terrible. I can't send that cake to school. What will people think? I know I can't bake. Why did I try? Everything I do fails. I will never bake again!" A mood of anger and frustration filled the kitchen.

As an outside observer, I took a chance and suggested a theme cake. "Why not put a sign on it that says, 'Grand Canyon Cake.'" This bit of humor helped my wife to change her inner dialogue. The cake was no longer a disaster. It was only an annoyance, and it did not have to be that. The mood changed, the cake was sent to school, and it did sell.

Observing Yourself

Paying attention to what you think means that you practice the process of self-observation. You try to catch your inner Voice as it speaks to you, asking, "What is it saying and is it helpful or not?" Learning to recognize an overly critical inner Voice is important.

Let's suppose that you have learned the value of making mistakes and have decided to quit criticizing yourself when you make one. If you try this process of self-observation, your first experience upon making another mistake will most likely be to become self-critical and hear your inner Voice saying, "Well, damn, you did it again. You criticized another mistake." You will have caught yourself after the fact and in the midst of negative reaction.

Whenever you hear your inner Voice saying, "Well, damn, you did it again," you should congratulate yourself. It is time for a celebration. You have made much progress because always in the past you would have listened to that negative inner dialogue and never even have known that you did it. You would think that it was normal. Progress is made when you are observant enough to catch what you are doing. Catching yourself after the act is good.

Now, just keep observing and soon the inner Voice says, "Here you are doing it again." But, you go ahead and do it. Nonetheless, more progress has been made because you are now finding yourself in the midst of the act. It is just that you are not yet able to stop.

Additional progress is seen when you hear the Voice saying, "Look out. You are about to do it again." Even as you proceed with self-criticism, you are slowly becoming more and more mindful. You are catching yourself in the act sooner and sooner.

Eventually, after a lot of hard work, you will hear, "Look out. You are about to do it one more time." At this point, however, you choose not to proceed. You don't begin the critical dialogue but intentionally initiate a positive one. You hear, "Mistakes are good. Now, I can learn. I'll try it again and see what happens." You are now breaking free of the negative thought pattern and consciously shaping your reaction to life events.

When you listen to your inner dialogue, catch it in action, and choose the more positive and realistic attitude, you are becoming a resilient person. Remember: your attitude is the key to resiliency.

Features of Resiliency

Daryl Conner in his book, *Managing at the Speed of Change*, lists five characteristics of resiliency.

♦ Be Positive: See life as challenging and dynamic and filled with opportunities.
♦ Be Focused: Determine where you are headed and stick to that goal so that barriers do not block your way.
♦ Be Flexible: When faced with uncertainty, open yourself to different possibilities.
♦ Be Organized: Develop structured approaches to be able to manage the unknown.
♦ Be Proactive: Look ahead and seek to actively engage change and work with it.

These resiliency features can be mapped on the Cycle of Change where they show us how resiliency helps at each step of the cycle.

The Six-Step Cycle of Change

◆ Being proactive enables you to prepare for what might be coming. It helps you to scan for signs of change at the step of sensing "Something's up." Once you get through a change, you need to again be proactive by looking ahead to what might be coming next and preparing to go around the cycle once more.

◆ Focus is needed to clarify the situation and clearly identify the problem or opportunity.

◆ Organization enables the development of a comprehensive, detailed plan of implementation.

◆ A positive outlook facilitates the actual beginning of the work of change as plans are put into action.

◆ Flexibility will be needed as adjustments are made, and you begin to sense that "this will work."

How well you handle and survive change ultimately depends upon how resilient you are.

Mismanaged Change

Mismanaged change is a common occurrence, and it leads to predictable results. These results are well captured in William Bridges' acronym of "GRASS." GRASS stands for guilt, resentment, anxiety, self-absorption, and stress.

Mismanaged change leads to feelings of guilt. Change can create survivors and losers. The survivors (perhaps those who stayed as others left in a downsize or layoff) often feel guilty for surviving. Managers, who had to make hard decisions about personnel changes, often experience guilt over the impact their actions had on others.

Resentment can be found up and down the organizational line as people make comparisons of "what" changed for "who" and find inequities.

Anxiety builds with the uncertainty of what will happen next. Anxiety is like a generalized fear, but unlike fear it has no specific object of focus. Anxiety is disruptive to concentration, attention, and efficiency.

Self-absorption comes about when all a person can think about is what will happen to "me." In periods of change, people become overly focussed on the limited sphere of how the change affects them.

Stress is the net result of the preceding factors, and it produces inefficiency and ineffectiveness while creating physical symptoms that lead to lost time at work and increased health costs.

Mismanaged change creates GRASS and the GRASS can grow very high.

People and Change

While controlling GRASS and managing change requires knowledge of the Cycle of Change and the Wheel of Life, it is essential to understand that successfully managing change is all about managing people. This central task is often resisted because in the midst of a difficult change there is a tendency to avoid that personal "touchy-feely stuff" of emotions. As one manager said to his staff, "It you want to have feelings, have them at home." This approach to change does not work, and the "people factor" cannot be overlooked. As noted by William Bridges, "First, you simply cannot get the results you need without getting into 'that personal stuff.' The results ... depend on getting people to stop doing things the old way and getting them to start doing things a new way. There is no way to do this impersonally."

Managing change is managing people, and when the needs of people are given appropriate attention, change goes more smoothly.

Managing people requires listening, empathy, and support as well as an openness to recognizing and engaging resistance. Everyone involved in making a change needs to be encouraged to provide feedback about the change process and efforts at creative problem solving should be encouraged and rewarded. When everyone understands the Cycle of Change and knows what to expect, both in terms of process and emotions, change goes more smoothly. In this supportive context of managing change, people are more easily able to move forward through the process toward a "new normal," and are more open to looking ahead to see what is already on the horizon.

The Cycle of Change and the Wheel of Life

Used in combination, the Cycle of Change and the Wheel of Life provide a complete model of the process of change. Together the two models help us to see that changes take place in three broad phases that William Bridges has labeled: (1) Letting Go, (2) Transition, and (3) Beginning.

Cycle of Change and Wheel of Life

Letting Go

What we call the beginning is often the end.
And to make an end is to make a beginning.
The end is where we start from.

~ T.S. Eliot

In order to change, we have to let go of "what was" to get to "what will be." "What was" is the state of normalcy before the recognition that "Something's Up." With the recognition of the need to change, we begin to sense the loss of what we have.

Change starts with loss. It begins with letting go. What this means to those who are leading change is that they should expect the initial emotional reactions of changing to be the typical reactions to loss, such as anger and grief. Worry, anxiety, and apprehension may also be present. To facilitate making a successful change, people must be allowed to do the work of letting go. Often this means that they must be educated in better understanding what is happening to them.

Being able to name a problem gives it a reality. Acknowledging that change begins with loss can help people begin to identify what they are experiencing. It also focuses them on what is being lost. Identified losses can range from relatively insignificant ones to major upheavals of life. The major losses are often clear, but people may need help in identifying the minor ones.

For example, you might be promoted to a new position and moved to a larger office only to find that you miss the view from the window in your former office. You might also miss the people with whom you worked. Or, you could move to a new home in the country, but miss the short walk to work that you had when living in the city.

Major losses could be of security, position, power, control, competency, or money. All of these losses (big and small) require acknowledgement and grieving before people can move forward to engage the change process.

Most of us have our typical way of approaching loss, and it can often be seen in the ways that we take our leave of "what was."

To discover your way of taking leave, recall jobs or relationships you have left. How did you do it? Did you follow one of the two typical but nonfunctional styles of leaving? Did you dash away or did you linger?

People who do not like saying goodbye leave as quickly as they can. They try to avoid the pain of letting go. They sever relationships, dash away, and as a result, leave loose ends.

People who linger will not leave. They hold on too long. They return too frequently. They are also trying to avoid the pain of loss. Neither of these styles is helpful.

A moderate approach is required. Loss leads to the normal emotions of sadness, regret, and anger, and an expression of these feelings of loss is needed. This process requires that a person experiencing loss be willing to talk and for the listeners to be empathic. Listeners may be family members, friends, co-workers, or the boss. Listening gives legitimacy to the feelings and may make them easier to bear. The facts of the loss do not change, but it is easier to go through the experience if you feel understood and supported.

When you are undergoing a significant change, pay attention to how you acknowledge your losses. Be sure to identify what you are losing and acknowledge it in some way. The better you understand what is lost, and the sooner you do the work of letting go, the quicker you can move on.

If you are trying to help others move through change, provide them with all the information you can about what is changing and what is not. Assist them in identifying and talking about the losses. Also, always treat the past with respect. Many people value the past and to belittle it creates resistance. Whenever possible try to offset perceived losses by helping people to clearly see what is being gained.

Consider providing some ritual or ceremony to help people relinquish "the way it was." This will help to clearly mark the ending and can enable people to move forward. For example, you could use a labyrinth walk where the journey to the center of the labyrinth symbolizes letting go. Or, people could write short descriptions of what they see as being lost that are gathered and given a ceremonial burial as a gesture of release.

Always be sure to establish the continuity of what it is that "really matters" and remains constant in spite of change. For example, in a hospital setting it will be the continuing focus on quality health care that remains primary. What is the essence of continuity in your setting?

Once people undergoing change are able to clearly understand and acknowledge their losses, they can move on to the stage of transition.

Transition

*Think of yourself as between trapezes when you have
let go of one rope but haven't grabbed on to the next.
The space is scary but also thrilling.*

~ Gail Blanke

On the Wheel of Life, transition is the process of
moving from Loss to Hope. Transition takes you
to the bottom of the Wheel and into Suffering, which is
the "living-through" phase of the change. On the Cycle
of Change, transition takes you from the step of "What
do I need to do?" to the step of "I will do this!"
Transition is the stage of planning, implementation,
and action. It is the longest and often most difficult
stage of change.

From a distance, change looks as if it quickly goes
from the "old way" to the "new way." It can be repre-
sented by a straight line divided into two segments
with an "X" marking the change.

<u>Old Way</u>　　　X　　　<u>New Way</u>

To an outside observer, it seems that the change is
announced and immediately implemented. A closer
examination, however, reveals that change is not
quick, and the "X" indicates a long period of planning,
preparation, and moving into the process. The reality
of change actually looks more like a classic growth
curve linking the old and the new.

The isolated "X" can be broadened into a large almond shaped area created by the overlapping of two circles representing the old and the new. This is the Zone of Transition.

Model for Transition

The "S-Curve" transecting the two circles begins to flatten as the old way has grown to the point where it is no longer working. Recognition and clarification of this fact leads to the experience of loss and letting go. The initiation of change moves into the Zone of Transition, which is often a surprise to those who were fully expecting to find themselves immediately involved in the new way of doing things.

Transition catches people off guard with its ambiguity and confusion and often creates a crisis-like atmosphere. Transition feels chaotic and people want to get out of it as quickly as possible. However, the chaotic nature of transition provides invaluable opportunity in that it opens the door to creative problem solving.

In the midst of transition, people have difficulty in accepting that loss, confusion, ambiguity, and chaos are normal to the change process. Helping people to deal with the stage of transition requires that it be normalized. Once people understand that they are responding in a normal manner, they are less distressed. Normalization begins by providing people with information. The more people understand the process of change, the better they can cope with it.

It also helps to explore the metaphors that spontaneously arise to express what is happening. Negative metaphors such as being caught like a "rat in a maze," "lost in the wilderness," or aboard a "runaway train" can siphon away needed energy and heighten frustration and hopelessness. Shifting to a more positive metaphor can be inspiring. Images of "leading a quest," "making a pilgrimage," or of "the little engine that could" can capture a new and invigorating spirit.

Central to successfully navigating through transition is the personal choice of an adaptive attitude toward change and life in general. A realistically positive attitude is a key feature of resiliency, and when people are resilient it helps them move through transition toward Hope and optimism. With the arrival of Hope, you have reached the stage of Beginning.

Beginning

There will come a time when you believe everything is finished. That will be the beginning.

~ Louis L'Amour

Once people have experienced and acknowledged the losses that come with change and have gone through the work of transition, they are ready to begin.

It is the work of letting go, clarifying the problem, creating a plan, and implementing it that brings you to the point where the change becomes a reality. With enough work, the momentum now exists to carry the change forward.

Continued adjustments may still be needed, but if everyone involved with the change has learned the "Four P's" of a good beginning, the process will go well. The "Four P's" are critical to success because they assure that people buy into the change. The "Four P's" are: Purpose, Picture, Plan, and Part to Play.

◆ Purpose: With a clear understanding of reasons for change, there will be a motivating purpose and goal.
◆ Picture: People need a picture (a mental image, an actual model, or a diagram) to give life to the process.
◆ Plan: A detailed plan of what will be done assures that the methods of reaching the goal are clearly understood.
◆ Part to Play: The specific role that everyone will fulfill in the change process is understood and accepted by all involved. People know how the change will affect them and the part that they will play in the change process.

The adoption of the "Four P's" by each person involved in implementing the change means that the change process has been well managed with a good use of the six-steps of the Cycle of Change and an empathic understanding of the emotions of change as shown in the Wheel of Life.

When establishing the Four P's, it helps to remember the four types of people and their different informational needs. We all have our favorite way of processing information and do better when we receive information in the way that we prefer. Some people are intuitive and like to see the "big picture" and grand scheme of how the change will work. They like to understand the "Why." Other people, who are sensory and detail-oriented, want to know the "What" regarding change. These people are action-focused and can move quickly once they know what needs to be done. Analytical people want to understand the "How" of change. They often like to take their time and mull over the plan for how things will work. "People-oriented" individuals tend to focus on the "Who" of change, and they wonder about the emotional impact that the change will cause and are concerned about how everyone will cope.

When introducing a change process, it is useful to address the issues of Why, What, How and Who so that all four types of people get the information they need in order for them to accept the Four P's, move forward, and begin changing.

Striving and Thriving:
The Challenge Continues

The daily challenge of facing change continues to escalate. The current rate of change shows no sign of slowing down. However, with knowledge of the Cycle of Change, the emotions of change, the value of resistance, and the importance of maintaining resiliency, we are empowered to more effectively design and implement change as well as to lead people through it.

We can do more than struggle to survive change.

We can strive with change by making the daily effort to actively engage whatever it brings our way. We can thrive on change by focusing our attention on realistic goals while maintaining a balance of meaning and purpose in our lives.

Remember: How we live with change is a personal choice. Make your choice one of striving and thriving.

Burnout Inventory

(Adapted from Freudenberger Burnout Scale)

Rate your risk for burnout. Read each question below and circle the number from 0-5 that shows how you have felt over the last three months.

1. Do you get tired easily? Do you feel worn out?

    0   1   2   3   4   5
No Change   Much Change

2. Do you get upset if people tell you, "You don't look so good lately"?

    0   1   2   3   4   5
No Change   Much Change

3. Are you working harder and harder and feel like you're getting nothing done?

    0   1   2   3   4   5
No Change   Much Change

4. Are you more sarcastic and disappointed in the world around you?

    0   1   2   3   4   5
No Change   Much Change

5. Are you sad a lot and don't know why?

    0   1   2   3   4   5
No Change   Much Change

6. Are you more forgetful (missing doctor visits, losing things)?

0	1	2	3	4	5
No Change					Much Change

7. Are you grumpy? More short-tempered? Do you expect more and more from the people around you?

0	1	2	3	4	5
No Change					Much Change

8. Are you spending less time with your friends and family?

0	1	2	3	4	5
No Change					Much Change

9. Are you too busy to do everyday things (make phone calls, send out cards)?

0	1	2	3	4	5
No Change					Much Change

10. Do you always feel bad, or are you sick all the time?

0	1	2	3	4	5
No Change					Much Change

11. Do you feel confused at the end of the day?

0	1	2	3	4	5
No Change					Much Change

12. Do you have trouble feeling happy?

    0   1   2   3   4   5
No Change   Much Change

13. Are you unable to laugh at a joke about yourself?

    0   1   2   3   4   5
No Change   Much Change

14. Does sex seem like more trouble than it's worth?

    0   1   2   3   4   5
No Change   Much Change

15. Do you have very little to say to people?
    0   1   2   3   4   5
No Change   Much Change

Add all of the numbers that you circled and the total is your score. Use the key below to interpret your results.

      0-25   You are doing fine.
      26-35 Watch out. You are at risk for burnout.
      36-50 You are a candidate for burnout.
      51-65 You are burning out.
      66+   Burned out. You may need to seek help.

References

Bridges, William. *Transitions*. New York: Addison-Wesley Publishing, 1980.

Bridges, William. *Managing Transitions*. New York: Addison-Wesley Publishing, 1991.

Conner, Daryl. *Managing at the Speed of Change*. New York: Villard Books, 1995.

Johnston, Daniel. *Lessons for Living: Simple Solutions for Life's Problems*. Macon, GA: Dagali, 2001.

Maurer, Rick. *Beyond the Wall of Resistance*. Austin, TX: Bard Books, 1996.

Woodward, Harry. *Navigating through Change*. Chicago: Irwin Professional Publishing, 1994.

Order Form

Striving and Thriving:
Meeting the Challenges of Change

Telephone orders: 478-471-1008

Mail orders: Dagali Press
                        5663 Taylor Terrace
                        Macon, Georgia 31210

Ship to:

Name: _____

Address: _____

City: _____ State: _____ Zip: _____

Please send: ____ books at $15.00 Total = $ _____

Shipping and handling   = $_____
(Add $3.00 for first book,
$0.75 per additional book)   Total = $ _____

Dr. Johnston is available for lectures and workshops.

For information write: Dagali Press
                            5663 Taylor Terrace
                            Macon, Georgia 31210

Call: 478-954-2460
E-mail: dan@lessonsforliving.com
Visit our Web site: www.lessonsforliving.com

Order Form

Striving and Thriving:
Meeting the Challenges of Change

Telephone orders: 478-471-1008

Mail orders: Dagali Press
                    5663 Taylor Terrace
                    Macon, Georgia 31210

Ship to:

Name: _____

Address: _____

City: _____ State: _____ Zip: _____

Please send: ____ books at $15.00 Total = $ _____

Shipping and handling   = $_____
(Add $3.00 for first book,
$0.75 per additional book)   Total = $ _____

Dr. Johnston is available for lectures and workshops.

For information write: Dagali Press
                         5663 Taylor Terrace
                         Macon, Georgia 31210

Call: 478-954-2460
E-mail: dan@lessonsforliving.com
Visit our Web site: www.lessonsforliving.com

About the Author

Daniel H. Johnston, Ph.D., is a clinical psychologist and former Director of Psychological Services at the Medical Center of Central Georgia in Macon, Georgia. He serves on the faculty of the Mercer University School of Medicine. Over the past 25 years Dr. Johnston has taught self-help skills to thousands of people in settings ranging from hospitals and clinics to community groups and churches. He is a frequent guest on local television and has had his own weekly show on 13WMAZ in Macon, Georgia.

Dr. Johnston has developed the popular Awakenings Web site (www.lessonsforliving.com) and offers information on psychological health to tens of thousands of worldwide visitors each year. He also is a columnist for the Macon newspaper, The Telegraph.

Printed in the United States
20278LVS00008B/18